Once Below
Bahamian

edited by
Telcine Turner

And once below a time I lordly had the trees and leaves
Trail with daisies and barley
Down the rivers of the windfall light.

Dylan Thomas, 'Fern Hill'

MACMILLAN
CARIBBEAN

Macmillan Education
4 Crinan Street,
London N1 9XW
A division of Macmillan Publishers Limited
Companies and representatives throughout the world

First published 1988 by
MACMILLAN EDUCATION LTD
London and Oxford
Companies and representatives throughout the world

www.macmillan-caribbean.com

ISBN 978-0-333-45835-8

2022
19

This book is printed on paper suitable for recycling and made from fully managed and sustained forest sources.

Printed and bound by CPI Group (UK) Ltd, Croydon, CR0 4YY

A catalogue record for this book is available from the British Library.

Contents

Dedication

To Mrs Lillian Coakley,
Southern Public Library,
New Providence, Bahamas,
for being Librarian,
and more.

Acknowledgements

I wish to express appreciation to the following who in some way contributed to this publication:

Of the College of the Bahamas — Mrs Ann Dean, for the encouragement to publish, and continuous support; Claire Belgrave, Mrs Marjorie Cheetham, Dr Joyce Johnson, Mrs Jacqueline Kennard, and Mrs Marjorie St Rose; staff and students of Willard Patton Primary School, T. A. Thompson Primary School, D. W. Davis Junior High School, C. I. Gibson Junior High School, and T. G. Glover Junior High School; Miss Verona Seymour, Language Arts Officer, Ministry of Education; persons in the community who shared their knowledge of Bahamian lore with students of ENG 122: Creative Writing; students of the mentioned course; persons whom I might have failed to mention; James O. Rolle, my husband, for his support.

Introduction

This collection consists of three kinds of short narrative: anecdotes from Bahamian lore, original nature myths, and Bahamian old stories, or folktales.

The stories under the heading of lore arose from a research exercise. Students had to research unusual events that truly happened to people who actually lived. In most cases the names of the persons involved in the happenings have been changed.

The myths were the result of an exercise whereby students wrote simple explanations, within a specific word limit, of particular human or animal characteristics or earth formations.

At present the Bahama Islands are in danger of losing a great part of their cultural heritage. With the exodus of many young and middle-aged islanders to the cities of Nassau and Freeport, many Out (now renamed Family) Island communities are becoming extinct. Much of the elements of the Bahamian lifestyle that originated in those communities is dying. Modern progress has dawned on the major Bahamian cities, but at the expense of burying our way of life. With the increasing popularity of television we are tending to adopt the speech and behaviour patterns and the value systems of the metropolitan societies to our north.

My feeling is that, in order to resist the imminent destruction of what it is that makes us Bahamian, we must seek to retain elements of the Bahamas of the past — hence the first type of stories. These attempt to record experiences that once, with the old stories, used to be transmitted by word of mouth.

The exercise of writing myths was intended to assure students that they possessed the needed ingenuity for creation of literature that children might enjoy.

Another part of the Bahamian oral tradition, the old story, has practically vanished in New Providence and must be near demise in the Family Islands. One of the anthropologists from the United States who researched the Bahamian old story earlier in this century, Daniel J. Crowley, noted in his publication that at the time he made his investigations Bahamians told such stories for entertainment, and to gain prestige. Nowadays, it appears, Bahamian entertainment comes in video-cassette packages, and personal prestige through ownership of a satellite dish.

Because I wish to record that we owned a folktale tradition I include here a retelling of three of the tales. In past pre-literate societies, as noted by May Hill Arbuthnot and Zena Sutherland in *Children and Books*, anthropologists found that folktales were once considered 'the cement of society'. They were used to reinforce the way people thought, felt, believed and behaved. The tales were used to promote kindliness, modesty, truthfulness, courage in adversity, and the conviction that eventually virtue will be rewarded; good will triumph over evil.

The storyteller, then, as well as being an entertainer, was the news-bringer and historian of the clan, prescriber and disseminator of his people's culture, upholder of their religious practices and their moral values.

Hopefully this collection will bring to classrooms a reminder of all the above attributes.

BAHAMIAN LORE

The Ghost in Mr Pratt's House

by
Toinette Major

My mother told me about the strange things that happened in the new house her father had just built when she was a child. She related the story to me once when I was a little girl. I was impressed and even frightened by the telling.

The Pratts were the big shots in Cabbage Point, Long Island. Mr Pratt owned the only vessel in the southern part of the island. He captained the vessel himself. In those days a trip to New Providence took fourteen days, one way. Everybody sent things with the captain to sell — maybe a sheep or goat. Then he had to buy flour, sugar, rice, etc with the money, to bring back. The young women plaited straw to buy cloth and shoes.

It was after Mr Pratt had built his big new house, which was close to the road overlooking the bay, that he went on a trip. His wife and thirteen children moved into the house. At that time there was no formal religious organisation on the island. A priest had never been in that settlement, so the house was not blessed.

In those days, only parents and older children

had the privilege of sleeping on beds. Those beds were not like the ones of today. They were stuffed with dry grass, and raised from the floor. The small children slept on grass pads on the floor.

My mother, Olga, was about seven years old at the time the events in this narrative took place. She slept on her small grass pallet on the floor beside her mother's bed. Her baby brother, Bruce, slept in her mother's bed.

One night Olga woke with the eerie feeling that something was wrong. Suddenly she knew what had caused her to awaken: she had heard something drop from one of the beams to the floor. The thing walked round and round her. Olga tried to call for her mother, but could not. She tried to move, but felt as stiff as a board.

At that moment the footsteps moved over to Olga's mother's bed. Olga heard a resounding spank, then Bruce's instantaneous squeal. In a flash Mrs Pratt had scratched a match from the box she kept under her pillow. They could see no one. For the rest of the night there was not another sound from their mysterious visitor.

On the following night the visitor came in through the door that led to the yard. Olga heard him pick up Bruce and begin moving back toward the door. It was only then that she could call out. Just as Mrs Pratt scratched the match, Bruce began to fall from about four feet in the air. He hit the floor-boards with a loud thump.

It was the next night that Georgianna, one of the other girls, felt something soft and fuzzy begin to move up her chest. When the thing started to feel her throat, Georgianna grabbed it with all her strength and threw it off. The thing fell on the neck of another girl, who had a stiff neck for a whole week afterwards. From then, Mrs Pratt kept a lamp burning at night until Mr Pratt returned.

When Mr Pratt heard about the strange happenings, he took some leather and put it into a smoke-pot. He then put the smoke-pot with the burning leather in the house. Then he closed all the windows and doors, with everybody outside. From that day onward the house was peaceful.

The Pratts later assumed that their house had been built on graves of slaves, since evidence showed that the property originally belonged to a slave-owner.

That Night in September

by
Phyllis Woodside

In 1968 in the settlement of Gambier, on New Providence Island, the following incident took place. The sister of Fred and Hezekiah told it to me.

One night in September, twenty-one-year-old Fred and his brother Hezekiah, aged nineteen, had just completed a visit with Matilda Rolle. When Fred told Hezekiah it was time to go, Hezekiah said, 'Holy smokes, man, Fred, you sure you wan' walk tonight? Le's stay by 'Tilda till mornin.'

'No,' replied Fred, 'you know we only came to visit. Furthermore, Mama and Papa gon worry if they don' see us home tonight.'

Still reluctant to go out into the darkness, Hezekiah said, 'Boy, it pitch-black. The moon gone sleep, aye? Well, le's go, then.'

They left Matilda's house after ten o'clock. As they walked the boys heard a long, moaning sound.

'What's that, Freddie?' asked Hezekiah.

'How I suppose to know?' replied Fred. 'Wait, man, that's a cricket. Yeah, that's a cricket.'

'If you say so,' replied Hezekiah.

They walked in silence for a few more minutes. Then something stopped them in their tracks, speechless. It was the soft crackling of bushes that moved when they walked and stopped when they stopped walking.

Both young men were frightened. They wanted to turn around to see what it was, but remembered the saying that if someone heard something

following him he should never turn around. Otherwise, whatever it was would come in front of him. This memory unsettled the boys further.

There was only one more mile to walk. As the brothers turned the last bend along that seemingly endless mile, a sight greeted their eyes that changed their walking habits from that day on.

Underneath a poinciana tree sat six midgets. Their faces were large. Their eyes looked as though they would glare out of their heads. The area in which they sat was illuminated by some strange force. This allowed Fred and Hezekiah to see the large jugs in the midgets' hands, and the smiles on their faces.

Fred and his brother ran from that spot as fast as they could. Then they heard the long, moaning sound behind them again.

Unable to restrain themselves, the boys looked back. Lo and behold, what should they see but the tallest, blackest man, clothed from head to toe in a white robe.

The brothers remembered nothing from that point: they fainted. When they came to, it was the following day. They were lying in bed at home.

Their father told them how he found them unconscious in the bushes, and how he had brought them home. Then memories rushed back to them. They related to their parents what they heard and saw.

As it turned out, at the time that the young men

were having those strange experiences their father was dreaming. He awoke screaming, but could not recall why he screamed. He asked his wife if the boys had arrived. When she said they had not, he instantly went looking for them.

Their father told them that a spirit had been following them. However, the spirit could not harm them, since their dead grandmother's spirit had also followed them. Their father never said how he knew this, but the young men marvelled at the implications of his words.

Since that night in September neither Fred nor Hezekiah walked anywhere after nightfall.

John Rolle

by
Marva Collins

This story was told to me by Mrs Rachel Ferguson, a native of Exuma Island.

On that island during the 1940s many stories spread about real-life encounters of humans with members of the spirit world. People of all ages lived in dread of walking alone at night along the unlit roads.

At that time in Rolleville, a settlement on Exuma, the majority of the men journeyed some twenty miles to Georgetown to farm. They left Rolleville at about nine o'clock at night in order to reach their farms early next morning. Not until the weekend would they return home.

The men were willing to walk this distance because the land in Georgetown was more fertile than that in Rolleville. They had little money, therefore they found it profitable to lease land from wealthy landowners. They repaid the lease by giving half their crops to the landowners.

John Rolle was such a farmer. He became famous on the island for his constant sightings of ghosts and jack-o-lanterns as he made his nightly journey to his farm. For this reason he always carried a sea-rod. These rods grew on the sea-bed, in the ocean. While in the sea they were smooth and flexible. When they were exposed to the sun for some time, however, the rods became extremely hard. Because of the hardness of the rods John Rolle felt that he could ward off any ghost. Other farmers sometimes walked with Mr Rolle but, characteristically, he preferred to walk alone.

On one particular night Mr Rolle walked very late. He had travelled some distance when he heard sweet music. A little surprised at first, he wondered where the music could be coming from. Since he could not find an answer he ignored the sound. Then he realised that a voice was speaking. The voice said, 'This is W.F.M., Spirit Time.' Although Mr Rolle was somewhat bewildered he was not really frightened. Thus he kept walking.

After John Rolle had travelled for about twelve miles he reached Farmers' Hill Bay. On the bay stood three men, naked except for their underwear. This sight piqued Mr Rolle's curiosity. He ran towards the bay. As soon as he reached the spot, however, the men disappeared.

By that time Mr Rolle was very much disturbed. Despite this he kept walking. After he had walked an additional three miles he reached Forest. Once again the voice spoke. It said, 'John

Rolle, meet me up under the big grape-tree.'

By then Mr Rolle had convinced himself that this was another farmer playing games with him. In the pitch-darkness of the night, however, he could see no one.

When John Rolle approached the grape-tree he suddenly found himself surrounded by ghosts. Immediately he tried to escape, lashing out wildly in all directions with his sea-rod.

The spirits retaliated by beating Mr Rolle. He realised that he was greatly outnumbered and he could not possibly defeat them. After a few minutes of struggling frantically to free himself, Mr Rolle fainted.

A few hours later, bruised and exhausted, he awakened, but could not find the energy to continue his trip. He succumbed to his injuries and fell into a tired, restless sleep.

On the following morning another farmer on his way to Georgetown found Mr Rolle. The farmer guessed what must have happened on the previous night. He carried Mr Rolle home.

Mrs Rolle was surprised and confused to see her husband. She ran to him and questioned him about his bruises. He then related the whole story.

News of old John Rolle's experience quickly spread throughout the island. After that encounter many people thought that Mr Rolle would no longer walk at night, but despite all that happened John Rolle continued his nightly walks. He became a local hero, and to this day Exuma Islanders consider him a brave man.

However, in spite of this farmers travelling between Georgetown and Rolleville avoided walking with John Rolle. They feared suffering the same experience.

Louis and the 'Chogers'

as told by Thelma Burrows
and written by Cindy Cartwright

The sun was making its descent on that seventh day of May, 1942, on the scarcely-populated island of Long Island. All of the chores on the Cartwright homestead were completed. The water-bucket was filled and placed along with a dipper in the window. The children's feet were scrubbed on the rocks and washed with Octagon soap, which had been washed ashore. The water-hole was emptied, rinsed, and sponged dry in preparation for the next day's scrubbing. The slop-bucket was placed behind the door of the master bedroom. All crocus-sack bedding was spread on the front-room floor in readiness for the children's bedtime. On the round mahogany table, which was covered by a floor-length table-cloth, the kerosene lamp was placed and lit.

Mama and Papa Cartwright were preparing to visit a sick neighbour who lived further down the road. The journey was made on foot, as there were no automobiles on the island, except a beach buggy which belonged to the Anglican priest.

Mr and Mrs Cartwright reminded the children to say their evening prayers, or else the soldiers would come and get them. It was during the Second World War. Parents used this fact to coerce children into completing chores to their satisfaction.

Sixteen-year-old Louis, who was naturally scary, and had a speech defect, was left in charge. After issuing strict instructions to the children to behave in the right way, Mama and Papa left.

With the door securely bolted and fastened, Louis began ushering the children under the solid hand-hewn table. Louis thought that there they would be safe from any intruders, whether they be human or ghost. With the children under the table Louis commenced with evening prayers.

When prayers were over the children began telling jokes and old stories. Laughing wildly, they failed to hear the sound of an approaching vehicle, but Louis, whose ears were tuned in to any irregular noises, heard. Shivering with fright he escorted the children outside to investigate. In the distance they saw a glare.

Louis said, 'Uh, uh, da chogers comin. Da chogers comin. Les go in the bushes.' Upon saying that he led the children into the bushes back of the yard.

The youngest child, a girl who was just turning four, was accidentally left behind. Her name was Vebee. Louis realised that she had been left, and went to lift her on to his shoulders. The children continued walking.

After about two minutes Louis realised that the child he was carrying was unusually heavy. He said, 'Gal, Vebee, you fat, hey? You mussie et too much grits.'

The child on his shoulders replied, 'Boy, dis ain't Vebee, dis Pearlie.'

Hearing this, Louis dumped Pearlie unceremoniously on the ground. Then he went back to get Vebee. It was that dark. Thus, it was difficult for Louis to see whom he picked up.

When the children reached the hills they looked down on the hollow and saw that the glare which they had seen was now stationed in front of their house. It was a huge ball of light. Louis giggled with satisfaction. 'I chode yinna cho. Da chogers watch goin get uch. We 'marter dan dem, doe, gal Pearlie.'

Soon the light moved away. Louis concluded that the 'chogers' must have gone to get their friends. 'I chode yinna cho. Les go back home.'

The children left their hideout. With Louis bringing up the rear, they returned home and hid once more under the table. They were just feeling comfortable when they heard footsteps. Their parents were returning.

Mr Cartwright asked them to come out from under the table. They did. Louis then related the story of how he secured the children in the hills from the 'chogers'. Mr Cartwright laughed. He told Louis that it had only been the priest who had come to visit the family. The priest also stopped at the neighbour's house and told Mama and Papa Cartwright that he had stopped by their house, but nobody was home.

Satisfied to know that it was not the 'chogers', the children crawled into their crocus-sacks and fell asleep.

Jack-o-Lantern

retold by
Isolene M. Rolle

It was about 10.30 p.m. They were some seven miles from Stafford Creek. Their hearts sang with joy as they sailed homeward. The night was pitch-black, the wind grease-oil calm; so calm that if one set a plate on the water the plate would float.

Velock and Raymond lowered the sail and proceeded to scull with an oar. Suddenly Velock shouted in surprise, 'Ole Ray! Ole Ray! Looka dere! Looka dere!' Raymond looked behind and there it was — a huge reddish-yellow blaze of fire on the water, coming towards the boat.

Velock and Raymond had been very close friends since childhood. They grew up in the community of Mastic Point, Andros. There they attended the all-age public school, a one-roomed concrete structure situated in front of the government dock. A two-bedroomed teacher's cottage was located to the north.

At age fourteen both boys had to leave school and go to work. Uncle Josh, Velock's stepfather, did not really accept the boy. He was sometimes unkind to him, so Velock had to work to help with living conditions at home. Raymond's father drank heavily. He squandered his money, so Raymond had to work to support his mother and the rest of the family.

When Raymond was twenty-three and Velock about twenty-four, each decided to look for a wife. Raymond did not have far to look, as he fell in love with Mootie, Auntie Mumma's daughter whom she had for Uncle Nezar. Velock won the heart of Minerva. She was the youngest daughter of a wealthy boat-builder of Stafford Creek, a little settlement about seventeen miles south of Mastic Point.

Whenever Velock wanted to see his intended he and Raymond would travel to Stafford Creek in a small dinghy. There they stayed with friends for a few days. It was on one of the nights going back that they saw a jack-o-lantern.

On seeing the blaze pursuing them the men

were terribly frightened. Raymond sculled faster. The faster the boat moved, the faster the blaze came toward them. Raymond slowed the pace of the boat; the fire-light slowed its pace. Raymond sculled at a furious speed, then stopped. The boat came to a standstill. The men noticed that their pursuer also stopped. Velock and Raymond felt so afraid at that time that their heads felt as heavy as giant pumpkins.

Velock took the oar. He sculled the boat at a normal speed. The light, which seemed to be getting bigger, slowed its pace to normal. In a hushed tone Raymond said to his friend, whom he had nicknamed Coley, 'Man, Coley, this mussie a jack-ma-lantern, ya know!'

Velock nervously replied, 'Ya think so, man?'

They said not another word until they were about one mile from their destination. Then they were aware that their follower had vanished.

Velock and Raymond arrived at the landing around three o'clock that morning. Now, each had to walk through a bushy track-road to get home. They decided to call out to each other until they reached their front doors. On they went, through thickets of bushes and over gravel paths. Raymond called at the top of his voice, 'Co-le-y! Co-le-y!'

Velock shouted back, 'Ole Ray! Ole Ray!'

The friends kept this up until Velock was safely inside his house which was nearer the landing than

Raymond's. From his house Velock could still hear his friend calling to him in the distance. Since that incident the men never left Stafford Cay after nightfall, when Velock went to court his intended.

Both men married. Each had twelve children. Velock became the minister of a Pentecostal church; Raymond became a deacon in a Baptist church. Raymond's wife died. Velock? One night, while preaching at a church convention to a large congregation that had gathered mainly to hear him, Velock collapsed and died. His wife, Minerva, still runs a small grocery store at Mastic Point.

On numerous occasions the friends told their children and grandchildren their experience on the night they saw a jack-o-lantern. They did this especially when they reminisced about the good old days.

Until the night Velock died he and Raymond remained the best of friends, so much so that people who knew of their relationship thought that after Velock's death, Raymond's would follow not far behind.

Hard-head Bird

by
Brendalee Conyers

Nicoll's Town, Andros in 1978 was a closely-knit community. One half of the population was related to the other, and the business of one person was everybody's business.

That summer I had recently turned eight. It was a local custom in Nicoll's Town for the younger children to go to the fields with grown-ups and older children during the summer vacation. I had to go to the fields with my grandfather and cousins. I was not needed to help harvest the crop. Instead, my grandfather gave me responsibility for tending to my two younger cousins.

The fields were located eight miles out of the settlement. They were cut up into sectors. This enabled the farmers to communicate among themselves. At lunch-time everyone gathered on a plot of land set aside for having lunch. During this rest period people socialised. They ate and gossiped about the latest news.

There was a farmer whose name was Gus. His field was located to the left of my grandfather's field. Anyone standing in our field could easily see anything that happened in Gus' field. So could the other adjacent farmers. This was so because of the closeness of these plots to each other.

Gus had been obsessed with love for his wife, Martha, when she was alive. Most of the men in the town laughed at Gus because of this obsession. Martha died giving birth to the couple's last daughter. Gus named the daughter Martha, after her mother. When Gus' wife died the obsession he felt passed on to his daughter.

Young Martha grew up very rude, selfish, and vain because of Gus' attention. He thought Martha could do no wrong. She was spoiled, since her father never disciplined her. He allowed her to have her own way in any matter.

Almost every other child over nine years old worked in the fields; all except for the invalids and Martha. Martha disliked working. Gus had fifteen children. He needed Martha's help, but he did not force her to work.

One particular day all the farmers went to the fields earlier than usual. They had to pick peas as soon as possible; otherwise, the sun would scorch the peas. That day I left my cousins with my great-grandmother; Grandfather needed me to help pick peas.

Although everyone was extremely busy, Martha, as usual, sat in a cool spot beneath two pine trees. At one point I heard her laugh hysterically. From where I stood I could see her,

but I could not see with whom or at what she was laughing.

Soon her father called from the far end of the field to ask what the joke was. She told him that an ugly bird kept flying around the pine trees. She was laughing at the bird. Everyone heard what Martha said. We all looked up to see the bird, but none of us saw it.

By lunch-time we were talking about the way Martha had acted. My grandaunt told everyone that she thought the spirit of Martha's mother had come to the girl. Martha, being the kind of person she was, had laughed.

However, one woman went to Gus. She told him that chickcharnies were half men and half birds. If a person saw them and laughed, they would punish that person. The woman also pointed out something else: chickcharnies built their nests where the branches of two pine trees joined at the top. Martha had sat under two such trees.

After Gus heard these things he went to Martha. He forbade her to go near the trees. Because she knew her father would not punish her if she disobeyed him, Martha still went to sit below the trees.

Towards the ending of the day we packed our farming tools and were about to leave the fields to go home when all of a sudden we heard a scream coming from Gus' farm. The older people told us to wait where we were and went to investigate.

Later my grandfather told us what they found out. Martha had screamed. He said that when they found her beneath the pine trees one of her knees was twisted away from her leg. There was a puncture in the middle of that knee. The puncture was full of straw. The older people took Martha to the clinic. The nurse called for an emergency flight from Nassau, and sent Martha on it to the hospital.

To this day Martha walks with a limp. When people ask her what happened that day in the fields, she always says that she does not know. The older folk still believe that as a result of her rudeness and disrespect to her father and the chickcharney Martha was punished. Hard-head bird don' make good soup.

Baa, Baa

by
Sheral Francis

It was a gloomy day in September, 1941 and no one in Clarence Town, Long Island was as sad as Laura. She was sixteen and unhappy because she had just found out that she was pregnant. She could not face her parents to tell them.

Laura decided to run away but she needed money. To get the money Laura stole three of her Uncle Sam's sheep, sold them, and left for Abaco. Sam was an alert man who watched his farm closely. He noticed that the sheep were missing two days after Laura left.

Late one evening Sam sneaked away to the next settlement. He went to an old man so that the man could fix[1] whoever stole his sheep. The old man lived alone in a small thatched hut near the beach. He would chant: 'Ten, ten, the Bible ten,' every hour, on the hour, to keep evil spirits away. He had no clock, but he accurately repeated that ritual every day.

Sam told the man his request. The man urged Sam to wait until midnight when he could begin to work on the thief of the sheep. At midnight the

1 put an obeah curse on

old man fidgeted with a worn out deck of cards. He rubbed oil in the design of a cross on Sam's forehead. Then he told Sam to strap a white piece of linen on all the remaining sheep's necks, and say the twenty-third psalm every night before he went to bed. After Sam heard the old man's instructions he went home.

By that time Laura was on the mail-boat, on the way to Abaco. The boat sailed near the western tip of Cat Island. Many people believed that the areas close to Cat Island were filled with evil spirits; that these spirits acted when called upon.

The old man and Sam had called on the spirits.

Someone in the boat mentioned that they were passing Cat Island. Immediately, Laura felt a terrible pain in her stomach. She moaned and groaned. Minutes later, to the astonishment of everyone, she went, 'Baa . . . baa,' like a sheep. This continued for hours until the boat had left the area of Cat Island. The experience was so strange that the captain decided to make an unscheduled stop at Eleuthera. There was a difference in Laura's behaviour; she was as peaceful as a lamb.

The next day on the boat was quiet. The only strange thing was that Laura had an enormous appetite. She craved cabbage and demolished a head of cabbage in minutes.

Eventually, to the relief of crew and passengers, the boat arrived at Abaco.

Laura settled in Hope Town with some cousins. Seven months later she gave birth to Melvina, prematurely. Melvina was not only very tiny, but vey unusual in other ways. It was impossible to get her to drink milk or juices. The only food that Melvina would eat was cabbage. Laura chewed the cabbage and gave it to Melvina. Melvina sucked on it with her tongue and swallowed it as an adult would, who had lost all her teeth.

This 'super-baby' drew people from all over the Bahamas. No one could understand her make-up, not even the doctors. Some people believed that

Melvina was abnormal because her mother and father were closely related.

When Melvina began to walk she did so with her head downwards. Her body grew in a bending position instead of upright. She continued eating a cabbage diet for twelve years.

On the night of Melvina's thirteenth birthday Laura had a dream. She dreamt about her family in Long Island, that her Uncle Sam was dying. On his deathbed Sam asked for his missing sheep. Then Laura remembered how she had sold the sheep. She recalled how she had behaved like a sheep on the boat.

She could take no more of the dream; Laura woke violently. The first thing that came to her mind was Melvina's physical condition. She ran to the girl's room. There lay Melvina, fast asleep. Laura felt reassured and strengthened.

On the following morning Laura tried to get out of bed, but she felt an awesome pain from her neck to her hips. She could not straighten her back. After trying for two minutes Laura managed to struggle out of bed.

'Melvina, Melvina,' she called, 'wake up. I have a bad pain in my back, and it look like it's bend over. Chile, go call Doctor and Rev.'

There was neither sound nor movement from Melvina. She was dead. The evil humped-back curse had passed from Melvina to her mother, on the same night that Sam died.

ORIGINAL MYTHS

Why Dogs Bark and Cats Meow

by
Carolyn Brooks

Many years ago there lived a dog, a cat and a wizard. The dog and cat could speak very well, but they never managed to hold a sensible conversation. Their attempts at being sociable always ended in arguments. Whenever they argued they did so at the top of their voices. The wizard who lived beside these two grew tired of their constant bickering. It disturbed him at his work. He decided to do something, so he made three plans.

First, he planned to invite the cat and the dog to a picnic by the sea. At the picnic he intended to push the cat into the water. Because the cat did not like water it would panic, and since the wizard himself could not swim the dog would have to rescue the cat. In that way the animals should become friends.

On Thursday of that week the wizard, the cat and the dog went on the picnic. After they had eaten the wizard suggested that they walk beside the sea. While they walked the wizard, in seeming accidental fashion, nudged the cat into the sea.

The cat instantly began screaming. The dog jumped into the water and saved the cat. The wizard thought this would make the cat grateful to the dog. Instead, the cat said to the dog that he had not needed his help; he could have swum out by himself.

'Why didn't you swim out, then?' asked the dog. 'And why did you scream so much?'

Thus started another argument. It took much effort on the part of the wizard to silence the animals. The wizard decided to use his second plan.

On Saturday of the following week the wizard hosted a slumber party, to which he invited the cat and the dog. He hoped that since those two would be sleeping under the same roof they would grow to like each other. The guests had a good time at the party. Even the cat and the dog seemed to be getting along. After much talking and laughing the animals readied themselves for bed.

In the middle of the night a terrible uproar woke the wizard. The cat and the dog were quarrelling again. The cat claimed that the dog kicked him while he slept. The dog accused the cat of continually pushing its paw into his mouth. They argued and argued. Although the wizard tried to settle the disagreement nothing worked.

At last the wizard resolved to use his magical powers. He put a curse on the pair. He said to the dog, 'Dog, from this day forth you will not talk; you will bark.' Then, to the cat the wizard said, 'And henceforth you will meow. If you meow and the dog barks you will not be able to understand each other. In that way you will quarrel less.'

From that day to this dogs bark and cats meow.

Why a Rainbow Comes after the Rain

by
Marjorie Dean

There was once a delightful little fairy who loved beautiful things. Her name was Rainbow. All the other fairies loved Rainbow because she was so attractive to look at. Her hair was light brown. Her skin was the colour of chocolate icecream. Her dark eyes seemed to look right into one's heart. Rainbow did not like gloom and ugliness at all.

The thing that bothered her most was the gray of the sky when it rained. It depressed her so much that she would cry and cry for days. Poor Rainbow would grow quite pale. She was already so small and fragile that the hysterics would make her sicker than ever. Therefore, whenever it rained all the fairies who loved Rainbow feared for her health.

Sometimes it rained for days. Then Rainbow would be almost unconscious from crying. The fairies knew that they had to do something, or they would lose Rainbow.

They called a meeting. At the meeting they made all kinds of suggestions about what to do.

None of the suggestions stopped the gray skies from forming after the rain. In despair the fairies gave up.

One fairy grew especially thoughtful. He could not forget how pale Rainbow turned when she cried. He badly wanted to do something about the situation, so he thought and thought and thought. Then the idea came to him: he would ask Rainbow why gray skies bothered her so much.

This the fairy did. Rainbow told him that she did not like gray skies because they seemed to represent the ending of everything beautiful. When she saw the skies change to gray she could think of no future at all. It was as if there *was* no future.

When the fairy left Rainbow he told the others what he had learned. They then resolved to find a way of showing a promise of a future after the rain.

Soon afterwards it began to rain. The rain continued for days. Rainbow wept again, but this time she became quite ill. The fairies feared for her life. They *knew* they had to do something. Then someone came up with a plan. They would paint the whole sky light blue, as far as the eye could see. Then, on the sky they would paint an arch made up of shades of yellow, blue, gold, green, and brown.

After the next rainfall the industrious fairies went to work. They worked for hours and hours. When it was done the arch was a most awesome sight. The fairies decided to call it a rainbow, for it represented all the beauty of Rainbow herself. When Rainbow saw their work she was overjoyed. She knew that every time she saw the bow she would think of a glorious future.

Why the Rooster Has no Teeth

by
Sheralyn McIntosh

Once upon a time the rooster had beautiful white teeth to help show off his masculinity. That was why he talked so much. No other animal had teeth like his. He never kept his mouth closed, but made a nuisance of himself by crowing all day and bragging about his teeth.

Then one day a little spoiled princess came along and saw the rooster. She had just that morning complained to her father of being bored with all the jewels in the kingdom — jewels like emeralds, pearls, rubies, and even the exotic jade. The rooster, of course, had his mouth open, so the princess saw his beautiful teeth.

'Oh,' she said, 'I must have one. It would make such a dainty ring for my finger.'

She went home and told her father. Although she was a spoiled child her father really loved her. He wanted to please her, for she was a good daughter at times. She curtsied at the appropriate moment. She hardly ever fussed for more than an hour when she was told to go to bed. And, too, it was her birthday.

The king ordered the rooster to be brought before him. How happy that rooster was to go, just to show off his beautiful teeth (to him the most beautiful in the world). But woe unto him. One of his teeth was ordered to be taken out, and the front one at that.

The chicken-dentist was sent for. A painful three days ensued when the reluctant rooster was strapped down and made to endure the torture of his first extraction. When it was all over he was sent on his way with nothing to show for his ordeal but a swollen mouth and injured pride.

The princess was overjoyed with her ring. She decided that she would have a necklace to match. Her father was obliged to give her her wish: it was Christmas, after all. Once again he sent for the rooster. This time all the teeth from the rooster's top jaw were taken out.

Even before the sorrowful rooster turned away the spoiled princess decided that she would also have a pair of earrings and bracelets to make a whole set. Thus there was a requirement for *all* the rooster's teeth.

The teeth made a lovely jewellery collection for the princess, but the rooster came away the most unhappy animal in the world, and certainly not the most comely.

From that day to this the rooster has kept his mouth shut. He has never bragged again and he only crows at dawn, when no one can see his empty mouth.

How the Bahamas Became an Archipelago

by
Pamela Carey

Long, long ago the Bahamas was one great big mass of land. It was a beautiful country. All its people, regardless of what section of the land they lived on, were known as Bahamians. The earth was very fertile. On it grew seagrape trees, guava trees, tamarind trees, mango trees, sugarapple trees, dilly[1] trees, and all sorts of other delightful fruit trees. The land was also filled with animals such as sheep, flamingos, goats, pigs, ducks, chickens, and a whole lot more.

Although the people were good at heart, they erected boundaries in the land. The different sections did not welcome visitors kindly. Each section had its own accent. There was much argument over which part of the country was the prettiest. The northern Bahamians claimed that the north was the prettiest. The central Bahamians thought that the centre was the prettiest. Likewise thought the southern Bahamians of their area. Little peace existed. An annoying, incessant murmuring could be heard day and night.

1 sapodilla

Now underneath the land mass lived a gargantuan creature called Nemo. He was over a hundred feet tall. He weighed more than any scale could tell. Nemo was usually a gentle, patient creature, but if driven he could do much damage. He did not bother anyone; therefore he did not like people bothering him.

Nemo loved quiet and so the constant noise made by the quarrelling Bahamians troubled him. Day in and day out he could hear the stupid people arguing. He thought the sound would go away. Instead it became worse. Finally Nemo could take the racket no longer. He climbed to the surface of the land. When the people saw him they were not afraid. They knew that he would not harm them.

Nemo calmly told the people to discontinue their argument about the beauty of the different areas. All the land looked the same to him. The Bahamians respected Nemo so they stopped their arguing. Nemo then returned to his underground home.

Then all the flamingos decided to go south and not come back. This caused more arguments and thus more noise. When Nemo rose for the second time he asked the flamingos why they left the other parts to live in the south. The flamingos said that the south was warmer.

'So there you have it,' Nemo shouted. 'The flamingos have a good reason for leaving. Now

shut up!'

His shout frightened the Bahamians. They decided to quit arguing. But the giant's raised voice also alarmed the crabs. Instantly the crabs fled to another part of the land and hid in holes.

The people in the segment to which the crabs fled gladly received them. On the other hand, those whom the crabs left fumed in anger. More disputes arose. At first they fussed in whispers. Then the disputing grew louder, and louder, and louder. Finally the group that the crabs had abandoned invaded the crabs' new homes. They beat the people there without mercy.

Once more Nemo rose from under the ground to investigate. When he saw the violence that once-gentle colossus flew into a rage. He grabbed the Bahamian land mass in both fists and broke it into some 700 islands, rocks, reefs and cays. These he set in the midst of a huge ocean. In that way the people in the different sections could neither see nor hear each other. Nemo made the portion on which the crabs lived the largest, so that he could sleep under it.

That was how the Bahamas became an archipelago. And if Andros could be lifted today you would see Nemo underneath, still fast asleep.

Why Human Beings Walk on two Legs

by
Carol Dean

Long, long ago, before the creation of hands there lived in the great land of Tomasi a rabbit named Kintoo, a spider named Jana, and a little boy named Buntwa. Buntwa's posture resembled that of the dog. He was bent over and walked on four legs.

These three friends lived together in a small hut away from all the other Tomasians. Kintoo was very quick. He hopped about on his two legs and helped greatly around the house. Jana was not so fast, but if someone asked her to do something, she did it. She crawled around on four legs. Buntwa was lazy. Even though he walked on four legs he felt that Kintoo and Jana could manage without his help. He did nothing but sleep. He woke only at mealtimes to eat what Kintoo and Jana had prepared.

Now, in the heart of Tomasi about a mile from the three friends' house lived King Ono. He was a great lion. King Ono ruled the land but unknown to many Tomasians he had magical powers. He used those powers when he was very pleased or very angry.

His Majesty's castle was almost completely destroyed by fire at one time. All the kind citizens of Tomasi pitched in to help repair the castle; that is, all except Buntwa. Every day before the sun rose Kintoo and Jana went to work on the castle. They returned home in the evening from a hard day's labour only to find that Buntwa had done no chores. The floor was still dirty. The beds were still unmade. Dirty dishes waited to be washed.

After several months the castle was restored to its former beauty. At that time King Ono ordered that everybody who had assisted in restoring the castle should sign his name on the royal register. In that way the king could thank his helpers.

When King Ono came to the hut of the three friends he checked his register. He then thanked two-legged Kintoo, the rabbit, by giving him two more legs. For her helpfulness Jana, the spider, was granted four more legs. They made her move faster. When King Ono saw that Buntwa's name was not on the list he questioned the rabbit and the spider.

'Your Majesty,' replied Kintoo, 'Buntwa does nothing but sleep all day.'

'He never helps anyone,' added Jana.

'Is that so?' said King Ono. At that moment Buntwa lay fast asleep on his bed with his four legs curled up beneath him. Right away King Ono resolved to use his powers to teach Buntwa a lesson. He poked the boy in his side. 'Wake up, you lousy little thing,' he said.

'Wha- What's happening?' asked Buntwa, dazedly. He felt annoyed at being so rudely awakened.

'You are going to be punished,' the good king replied. 'Stand on your feet at once!'

Buntwa rose from the bed and did as he was told. He did not look at his friends.

The king chanted in his deep voice:

Winkleton dimbledee
A la ma fesson.
Master of Zol,
Teach this slow boy a lesson!

Instantly Buntwa felt his body becoming straight. He stood on two feet. The limbs that had been his other legs now hung from his shoulders.

'As of today, Buntwa,' said King Ono, 'you will walk on two legs. You will use your hands to help others as well as yourself. Or do you want to be punished again?'

'No, no, sir. I mean — Your Majesty,' Buntwa stammered. 'I'll never be lazy again. I promise.' Right away he began to do housework.

Then the king bade the friends good-day and left. From that day to this human beings have walked on two legs.

Why the Octopus Moves Backwards

by
Isolene M. Rolle

Softy was an octopus. She always thought of herself as being graceful, the most graceful and prestigious animal in the sea. She looked on the other animals such as Crawfish, Conch, and Starfish with scorn. She counted the smaller animals — Chiton, Squid, and Oyster — inferior. One day Softy's attitude changed. She came to realise that the other animals were just as important as she. What was more, they were just as wise and alert as she thought herself to be.

It happened like this. Softy had been taking her usual stroll. She moved with dignity and pride along the ocean bed. Whenever she met other animals whom she did not like, or whom she thought little of, she squirted her poisonous ink. The ink clouded the surrounding water. In many instances it killed younger, more helpless animals. Softy's actions upset many sea animals because she killed several of their babies.

The animals elected to do something about the problem. They would teach Softy a lesson that might cause her to change her improper attitude.

Crawfish co-ordinated the plan. A meeting was called for very early one morning, before Softy awoke. After the meeting the animals went about setting their plan to work. They worked in groups. The groups were made up of the smallest animals. They waited for the signal from Crawfish, who served as the watch to see when Softy appeared.

Crawfish spotted Softy coming in their direction. He signalled the groups to move teasingly across Softy's path. Said Little Bleeding Teeth (a small shellfish) as she bounced off the rock in front of Softy, 'This is the day we will take revenge on you.'

The animals came from all directions. They made a dense circle around Softy. Shocked and confused, Softy wondered where these little fellows had mustered such courage. When she caught on to what was happening and tried to escape she found there were too many little sea animals enclosing her around.

Softy attempted to kick her way through the crowd, but a large number of the animals pounced on her. Their attack caused her to unbalance. Over and over she tumbled. Just as Softy resolved to squirt her substance on the animals seven jellyfish arrived. The jellyfish spurted their purple fluid over Softy from seven directions. It was the first time she had seen such a thing. Softy was too startled to respond.

In seconds the water around her grew purple. Softy could not figure out where to go. Every time she moved forward she hit into one animal or the other. The animals blocked the shoal in which Softy wanted to take refuge. When she looked up Softy saw that the water was an even darker shade of purple. That meant that the jellyfish had her trapped from the top also.

A contingent of starfish placed their bodies in such a way that their legs stuck out in front. They intended to block Softy from all sides. Softy looked at them and thought, 'If starfish can move like that I should be able to do so. I could even move at a faster pace, because I have eight legs. Starfish have only five.' She knew that if she did not get out of her predicament quickly she would be dead in seconds. Softy glanced behind her. There was a gap between two starfish, so she seized her chance.

With a sudden backward jerk Softy parachuted through the small opening. Her speed was so great that none of her enemies could catch up with her.

Ever since that day Softy, the octopus, has been parachuting backwards. She realised how much speed she could make by travelling in that position. It was safer to move that way than to spread all eight legs in all directions, she decided. From that moment on the octopus has moved backwards.

BAHAMIAN OLD STORIES

The House in the Sky

a Bahamian old story retold by
Telcine Turner

Once upon a time there lived two friends — a goat named Brer Booky and a rabbit named Brer Rabby.

At one time, life in the area where they lived was rough. Brer Booky could hardly find food for his family. On the other hand Brer Rabby's household looked plump and prosperous. One day Brer Booky went to his friend. He said, 'Brer, how come me and my family catching so much hell, and you and yours looking so well?' Brer Rabby just laughed.

Because Brer Booky persisted with his questions Brer Rabby finally gave in. He said, 'At day-clean tomorrow bring a bag 'round by my house. Then we'll go to my food source.'

That night Brer Booky could scarcely sleep. He was so impatient that he rose early, heaped dead branches in the east near Brer Rabby's bedroom window, lit a fire and crowed, 'Cock-a-doodle-doo! Cock-a-doodle-doo!'

Of course when Brer Rabby awoke he was

annoyed to see a false sunrise at four o'clock in the morning.

Finally, the friends set out for the food source. They walked and walked for miles. Brer Booky was feeling the direct heat of the mid-morning sun when Brer Rabby stopped short under a seagrape tree. Brer Booky wiped sweat from his face and looked around. He saw nothing marvellous.

Brer Rabby said, 'Now, Brer Booky, listen well 'cause I'm only going to do this once.'

He sang:

> 'Marry, come down low,
> Marry, come down low,
> Marry, come down low
> 'Til you touch the ground.'

To Brer Booky's astonishment a neat clapboard house descended from the sky. Brer Rabby said, 'Open, Kafeysha, open!' Instantly the front door flew open. A dazed Brer Booky followed Brer Rabby in. Then Brer Rabby sang the house up.

Brer Booky grew more dazed when he saw the food: peas and rice, fried goggle-eyes, stewed conch, crab and rice, peas soup and dough, coconut tart, benny cake, soursop icecream, lemonade — all in endless supply. While Brer Rabby stuffed food into his bag, Brer Booky stuffed his stomach. He ate and ate and ate.

Eventually Brer Rabby turned to go.

'Go?' yelled Brer Booky. 'Go, and leave all this

wonderful food? No, no. You go, I'm staying right here.'

Brer Rabby tried to persuade his friend to leave, but at last gave up. 'All right, Brer Booky,' he said, 'only don't forget how to get out.' With that Brer Rabby sang the house down, commanded the door to open, and left.

Gladly Brer Booky sang the house up again and continued his fiesta. So busy was he that he did not realise that the house was going down once more until he felt the floorboards shake under his feet. Fear overtook Brer Booky. What would the occupants of this magical house do to him if they found him there? Brer Booky scrambled under the bed as he heard a voice sing in a nasal tone:

'Marry, rise up high,
Marry, rise up high,
Marry, rise up high
'Til you touch the sky.'

From under the bed Brer Booky could see the legs of the family who lived in the house. There was a mama ghost, a papa ghost, and a little girl ghost.

Now a custom of ghosts, or 'sperrits', as they are known in the Bahamas, was to take off their heads whenever they went to bed. Therefore, before the papa ghost lay down he hung his head on a nail. The mama ghost proceeded to feed the little girl, who sat on the floor by the bed, directly in front of Brer Booky's hiding-place.

As the girl ate Brer Booky kept nudging her. 'Gimme some, gimme some,' he asked. 'Give your papa some!' He did this again and again. Again and again the child begged her mother for more food.

At last the mama ghost said, 'Marylou, what wrong with you? All of a sudden you get so much appetite.'

The girl chanted:

'I gat two daddies:
One in the bed
Ain' gat no head;
One under the bed,
And he eyes shine like a dollar!'

The papa ghost jumped up. 'What you say, Marylou?'

The girl repeated:

> 'I gat two daddies:
> One in the bed
> Ain' gat no head;
> One under the bed,
> And he eyes shine like a dollar!'

Instantly the papa ghost pulled Brer Booky from under the bed. What a great struggle then took place. Brer Booky wrenched free. He jerked this way, lurched that, dashed and whirled and twisted and twirled until it would have made a person light-headed to watch him. Wherever he dashed the ghosts followed.

Brer Booky darted for the door but could not remember the formula that would open it. Taking pity on Brer Booky, the little girl said. 'Big man like you can't say "Open, Kafeysha, open"?'

The door burst open. Out fell Brer Booky and down, down, down, right into the topmost branches of the grapetree. It was a wonder that he landed without breaking every bone in his body.

When Brer Booky reached his house his wife met him with the broomstick. As he felt the thwack! thwack! thwack! of the stick against his skull Brer Booky was sorry that he had not suffered any broken bones.

The Simpleton

a Bahamian old story retold by
Telcine Turner

Once a widow had a son named Claude. He was mannerly but never seemed able to do anything right. His mother feared for her old age.

The day Claude said he was going to seek his fortune his mother's fears increased. She tried to change his mind, but the boy *would* go. The mother packed a loaf of bread, a bottle of water, and said , 'Son, always be mannerly. Manners take you through the world.' Then she blessed Claude and sent him on his way.

Claude walked and walked all that first day and well into the next. By evening he was without food. He decided to stop at a small hut on the outskirts of a huge forest. The hut belonged to an old woman who had magical powers, but Claude did not know that.

'Mother,' Claude said, 'I'm a tired traveller seeking his fortune. May I rest here tonight?'

The old woman agreed.

She showed Claude to a lumpy mattress. That night he spent in turmoil: scorpions stung him; snakes twined around his limbs; mosquitoes sang in his ears. Yet when the woman asked how he had spent the night, Claude replied, 'Very well, mother.' This politeness impressed the old woman, but she decided to test Claude further.

'Son,' she said, 'I'm going on an errand. A black cat will soon come around. Beat it and chase it off!' This the old woman did to test whether Claude would obey in spite of what his conscience told him was the right behaviour.

No sooner had the woman left than the cat appeared. It was ugly and mangy, looking and smelling as though it had not cleaned itself within a year. But it meowed so piteously that Claude gave it most of his breakfast.

When the woman returned she asked if the cat had come. Claude merely nodded. She knew what he had done, for the black cat was one of her disguises. Again she felt pleased. Still, the woman decided on a final test.

She said to Claude, 'Bring me three pumpkins from yonder field. Do not pick those that cry out, only those that are silent.'

Claude entered the field. Immediately several plump jolly pumpkins shouted, 'Pick me! Pick me!'

Claude looked around. The silent pumpkins were small and measly-looking. For a moment the fat pumpkins tempted Claude but he resisted the thought. He took three silent, undersized pumpkins.

The old woman was delighted, as the last test showed that Claude was above being greedy. As Claude was leaving she gave him the pumpkins. 'Son,' she said, 'you have been considerate and modest. Take these. Any time you face danger or are bewildered toss one down. They will lead you to your fortune.'

Claude did not know what to make of her last remark. The woman concluded, 'May good go before you and bad behind.'

The youth continued on his way. As he travelled deep into the forest he heard a tremendous roar. It seemed to come from all around him. Claude turned. A giant beast was hurtling towards him. What could he do without a weapon? Then he recalled the woman's gifts.

Directly Claude threw down a pumpkin a spear leaped into his hand. He downed the beast with one lunge. Feeling confident, he continued his quest.

Further and further into the forest he tramped. Presently he noticed that the path had grown fainter. Soon it vanished altogether. Claude stopped and looked around. All he could see were trees. They seemed to be closing in on him. His heart thumped like a drum in his chest. He was lost, miles from anywhere. But before fear could make a true idiot out of Claude he remembered the pumpkins. He threw down one. Instantly a road shone like a silver ribbon through the forest.

Claude followed the road. It led to a splendid estate with miles of acreage, every fruit tree imaginable, crops ready for the picking, wonderful plants, exotic flowers, and healthy and plentiful livestock.

He rapped on the door of the mansion. Nobody answered so he went in. What a sight met his eyes: towering walls, glass ceilings, ornate tiles, elegant furnishings. But where were the people?

In the midst of his puzzlement Claude thought of the last pumpkin. He tossed that down. The scene that emerged was a picture of bridal festivities. There were men and women resplendent in pastel-coloured suits and gowns. Claude stood rooted and stared at the company.

Then a young woman in an exquisite white dress came towards him. Blue forget-me-nots formed a coronet for her veil. She pushed back the veil and said, 'We have been waiting for you.'

In that moment Claude understood what the old woman meant when she said her gifts would lead him to his fortune. He married the young woman. For all we know, he still lives happily with his wife and mother on that splendid estate.

How Brer Rabby Tricked Brer Lion

a Bahamian old story retold by
Telcine Turner

Whew! I'll show that bigoted rabbit I can take care of myself, thought Brer Booky. Imagine him telling a sensible goat like me I'm bad luck; that I'd better not tag along when he goes hunting. I'll show that Brer Rabby. Just after I drink some cool water from this well.

'Hello, up there!'

Brer Booky looked around. He did not see anyone. Could the voice belong to a ghost? 'Where are you?' asked Brer Booky.

'In the hole.'

The nearest thing to a hole that Brer Booky could see was the opening of the well. He peeped over the edge. 'Who's there?'

'Brer Lion. I've been here five days without food. Get me out and I'll reward you beyond thinking.'

Brer Booky smiled at the thought. 'Brer Booky at your service. I'll have you out in no time.' If he freed Brer Lion that would show Brer Rabby that he could be a useful friend.

Four hours later Brer Lion climbed to freedom on Brer Booky's branch-and-vine ladder. He shook his damp rump, spraying water all over Brer Booky. Then, to Brer Booky's surprise, Brer Lion lurched toward him, growling. 'Now, I shall eat you!'

'But I set you free, and you promised me a reward beyond thinking.'

'Eating you *would* be a reward beyond thinking,' said Brer Lion.

'Please, Brer Lion,' said Brer Booky, 'you waited five days. You can wait one hour more.'

Brer Lion sharpened his claws on a tree-trunk, a sight which frightened Brer Booky intensely. 'Find food for me or I shall eat you,' roared Brer Lion.

With that he marched into the forest with Brer Booky ahead of him.

On the way they met Brer Dog. 'Oh, Brer Dog,' Brer Booky said, 'I rescued Brer Lion from a deep deep hole. Do you think he should eat me?'

'I would,' yapped Brer Dog.

'Get ready,' snarled Brer Lion. 'I am going to eat you.'

'Brer Lion,' pleaded Brer Booky, 'you waited five days. You can wait thirty minutes more.'

They travelled on and met Brer Frog. 'Oh, Brer Frog,' said Brer Booky, 'I rescued Brer Lion from a deep deep hole. Do you think he should eat me?'

'I would,' croaked Brer Frog.

'Now, are you ready to be eaten?' roared Brer Lion.

Tears dripped down Brer Booky's cheeks. 'Please, Brer Lion,' he begged, 'you waited five days. You can wait a few seconds more.'

Brer Lion stomped his feet in anger; all the leaves fell from the trees. 'This is your last chance, Brer Booky,' he said.

On they travelled and met Brer Rabby. At the sight of his friend Brer Booky's heart danced. 'Oh, Brer Rabby,' he said, 'I rescued Brer Lion from a deep deep hole. Do you think he should eat me?'

Brer Rabby said to Brer Lion, 'Your Supreme Majesty, I am disappointed that you should consider dining on such a worthless creature.'

To Brer Booky Brer Rabby said, 'You think I

was born yesterday? That I would believe a scrawny, dull-witted goat like you could save anyone? You will have to prove it.'

Brer Booky trudged half-heartedly back to the hole with Brer Lion and Brer Rabby.

Brer Rabby looked at the ladder and called it a paltry contraption. He said to Brer Booky, 'You silly goat. Do you think I would believe such a flimsy structure can bear the weight of His Majesty?'

At Brer Rabby's insult anger surged inside Brer Booky. 'My ladder *did* save His Highness!' he shouted. 'And don't call me silly, or else -' He rushed toward Brer Rabby but Brer Lion came between.

'No need for violence,' said Brer Lion. 'I can solve this problem by eating you right now.' With that Brer Lion lunged at Brer Booky.

'I beg of you, stop, Royal Sire,' said Brer Rabby. 'Surely this lying, good-for-nothing creature is unworthy of the regal appetite.'

'After five days without food anything would be worth eating,' growled Brer Lion. 'Still, to prove the truth of this goat's story and that he deserves to be my next meal, I shall demonstrate.' With that Brer Lion climbed into the hole.

In an instant Brer Rabby pulled up the ladder. He shouted down to Brer Lion, 'How long did you say you were in there?'

'Five days,' called Brer Lion from his prison.

'You can stay there five days more!' said Brer Rabby. That was how he tricked Brer Lion.

Questions and Activities

THE GHOST IN MR PRATT'S HOUSE

Questions

1. How did the people of Cabbage Point pay for the foodstuffs that Mr Pratt purchased in New Providence?
2. Who, in Nassau, do you think bought the straw that the young women of Long Island plaited?
3. What do you understand 'blessing' a new house to mean?
4. What did Mrs Pratt do, finally, to keep their strange visitor away?
5. Why did Mr Pratt smoke out the house?

THAT NIGHT IN SEPTEMBER

Questions

1. Even if you didn't know their ages you might be able to guess, from reading the story, that Fred is older than Hezekiah. How?
2. The midgets whom the brothers saw did not seem violent or unfriendly. Why, then, were the brothers so afraid?
3. What made the boys' father go in search of them?
4. Have you or anyone you know seen a ghost? What was the experience like?

JOHN ROLLE

Questions and suggestion for activity

1. On that special night why did John Rolle think another farmer

was playing games with him?
2. Do you agree that John Rolle was brave? Why, or why not?
3. Why do you suppose Mr Rolle preferred to walk by himself?

Imagine yourself being at the Rolle house when John told his wife of his strange experiences. Make up the dialogue between the two.

LOUIS AND THE 'CHOGERS'

Questions and suggestion for activity

1. What preparations did the Cartwright family make for bedtime?
2. How do the preparations we make before going to bed differ from what the Cartwrights did in 1942?
3. Especially on what used to be called the Out Islands, there used to be a superstition that a family should never retire for the night and leave the water-buckets empty. What was the reason for this belief? If you don't know, guess.
4. Do you know anyone who has trouble pronouncing certain words, or anyone who has difficulty speaking at all? How do you think we should treat such persons? Why?

Say the following speech of Louis in normal, properly-pronounced English:

> 'I chode yinna cho. Da chogers watch goin get uch. We 'marter dan dem, doe, gal Pearlie.'

JACK-O-LANTERN

Questions

1. Why did Velock and Raymond have to leave school at an early age?
2. When the writer says 'when Velock went to visit his "intended" ' what do you think she means?
3. Why do you think both Velock and Raymond chose careers in the church?
4. At the end of the story a belief regarding close friendships is mentioned. What is it?
5. Do you think this belief is true? Explain.

HARD-HEAD BIRD

Questions

1. What kept Gus from asking his daughter, Martha, to help on their farm?
2. There were two explanations concerning the identity of the bird at whom Martha laughed. What were the explanations? Which do you agree with? Why?
3. Do you think Martha should have been punished? Why, or why not?

BAA, BAA

Questions

1. Why do you think the old man waited until midnight to begin working obeah?
2. Why was Laura peaceful when the mail-boat stopped at Eleuthera?
3. Fairly early in the story we are given hints that Melvina will be an abnormal baby. What are the hints?
4. Based on the events in the story, what kind of person do you think Sam was?
5. What kind of person do you consider Laura to have been?
6. Do you think people should work obeah on one another? Why, or why not?

WHY DOGS BARK AND CATS MEOW

Questions

1. How did the wizard first plan to make the cat and dog become friends?
2. Why did that first plan fail?
3. What is a slumber party? Was that a good idea for the second plan?
4. If this myth were true would you say that the wizard's third plan worked? Why, or why not?

WHY A RAINBOW COMES AFTER THE RAIN

Questions and suggestion for activity

1. What troubled Rainbow most? Why?
2. How did the fairies discover what it was that bothered Rainbow?
3. The fairies intended the pretty colours in their bow to mean something special to Rainbow. What was that something?

Draw and colour a picture of Rainbow, keeping in mind the way that the writer described her.

WHY THE ROOSTER HAS NO TEETH

Questions and suggestion for activity

1. Why did the king decide to give his daughter a ring made from one of the rooster's teeth?
2. What was the king's reason (or excuse) for giving the princess a rooster-teeth necklace?
3. What two items of jewellery were made from the last of the rooster's teeth?

Separate into groups. Let each group practise performing various sections of the story where the rooster is called upon to give up his teeth. Each group can perform before the class. Class members can comment on the performances and perhaps three groups can present the story in pageant form, with a good reader reading the narrative portions.

HOW THE BAHAMAS BECAME AN ARCHIPELAGO

Questions

1. Besides 'gargantuan creature' two other words are used separately to refer to Nemo's huge size. What are these words?

2. What is the name of the island in the southern Bahamas to which the flamingos went? It has six letters.
3. The section of the Bahamas to which the crabs fled would now be known as ______Island.
4. From your knowledge of the Bahamas, would you say that the various islanders speak with the same accent? Explain.

WHY HUMAN BEINGS WALK ON TWO LEGS

Questions

1. What chores did Buntwa leave undone, when Kintoo and Jana went each day to help rebuild the king's castle?
2. When King Ono told Buntwa to stand, Buntwa did so without looking at his friends. Why?
3. Did the king's spell have the effect he wanted to achieve?

WHY THE OCTOPUS MOVES BACKWARDS

Questions and suggestion for activity

1. What does the name 'Softy' suggest about an octopus' body?
2. Why did Softy mistreat the crawfish, conch, starfish, chiton, squid and oyster?
3. How did the animals take revenge on Softy?

Make up a game showing how the smaller sea animals imprisoned Softy. For example, the class can break into circles of five students each, with one person in the centre of each circle.

The aim of that person would be to escape. The aim of the others on the edge of the circle would be to keep the person in. Make up your own rules.

THE HOUSE IN THE SKY

Questions

1. From the way he acted with the food, what kind of personality did Brer Booky have?
2. How did the character of Brer Rabby differ from that of Brer Booky?
3. Why do you think the girl gave food to Brer Booky?
4. Why did the girl give the door-opening formula in the way she did?
5. If Brer Booky had suffered broken bones do you think his wife would have behaved differently at the end?

THE SIMPLETON

Questions and suggestion for activity

1. Why was Claude's mother fearful when he told her he was going to seek his fortune?
2. Why do you think the old woman gave Claude the lumpy mattress?
3. How did Claude show that he was considerate to the old woman?

Form groups of about five persons each. Now separate and make up an explanation for the mansion being empty. When you meet as a class, have a spokesman from your group tell the class your group's explanation. You may also make a play from your story.

HOW BRER RABBY TRICKED BRER LION

Questions and suggestion for activity

1. Why was Brer Booky frightened at the sight of Brer Lion sharpening his claws?
2. On the way back to the hole Brer Booky felt sad. Why?
3. What was clever about the way Brer Rabby tricked Brer Lion?
4. Do you think that Brer Booky acted wisely or foolishly in the story? Explain.
5. If you had been Brer Booky, would you have helped Brer Lion?
6. Do you know of anyone who was ungrateful to the person who helped him or her?

The story lends itself to dramatisation by groups. In fact, a different group (three persons) can perform each of the sections in the story where Brer Booky appeals for justice. Another group might act out the end, where Brer Lion returns to the hole.

References

Children and Books, May Hill Arbuthnot and Zena Sutherland. Scott, Foresman and Company, 1972

I Could Talk Old Story Good: Creativity in Bahamian Folklore. Daniel J. Crowley. University of California Press, 1966

Folk-Tales of Andros Island, Bahamas, Elsie Clews Parsons. The American Folkore Society, 1918